PROGRAM EVALUATION

in
church
organization

PROGRAM EVALUATION

in
church
organization

by

M. James Gardiner, Ph. D.

Second Printing August 1977

Library of Congress Catalog Number: 77-80070

International Standard Book Number: 0-89305-017-2

Printed in the U.S.A.

*For Marilyn, whose love and understanding
provide the springboard
for all of life.*

TABLE OF CONTENTS

PREFACE

This book is written with one goal; to help persons within church organizations make informed decisions about program activities. Everyone who works within the structure of the church has, at one time or another, had questions about the value and feasibility of the organization's programs. This book is an effort to aid in arriving at meaningful answers to such questions. This book is directed toward the needs of those persons who are the day to day managers of the church's activities. As such, it is not a book of theory. Instead, it is a book which sets out the necessary and practical steps for any program evaluation accompanied by explanations of how and why these steps should be taken.

The reader will notice the lack of footnotes within the text. However, I have to acknowledge an intellectual debt to many who have taken the time to write of their painstaking and sensitive work in the area of evaluation. The selected bibliography appendixed to this work is such an acknowledgement. I am grateful to those who helped me in my struggles to grasp a limited understanding of the evaluation process — in particular, Professors Al Lindgren, Charles

Thompson, Gus Rath, the students in my classes and to the leaders of other churches in which I was allowed to sharpen my skills. A special debt of gratitude is owed to Professor Robert C. Worley, who gave me the opportunity to study, the encouragement to endure and the freedom to test my wings. To a large degree, it is he who has made this writing possible.

Orlando, Florida 1977

M. James Gardiner

Chapter I

EVALUATION IN CHURCH ORGANIZATIONS

Efforts to evaluate programmatic activities are as numerous as prolific social programs of our times. The government uses evaluation as a basis for granting funds to proposed new programs and for perpetuation of grants to continue ongoing programs. Educational institutions are using evaluative methods both to determine the effectiveness of educational programs and to measure the effectiveness of the educators.

The word, evaluation, is now among the common parlance of the denominational churches. Many programs must have built-in evaluative modes in order to secure operational budgets. Several denominations have institutionalized an office of evaluation. There are classes on evaluation being taught in seminaries.

With all of the evaluative activity being carried forth there is little evidence that the information surfaced has been effective in bringing about productive organizational change. Church organizations are still struggling with insufficient programmatic support; they are still having to replace personnel who have been employed to do a required task but, after a short period of working, find they are not equipped to accomplish the assignment; programs are still being duplicated, new programs are replacing non-functional existing programs, and are time and again falling short of the hoped for goals.

In this day we are finding more and more programs competing for scarce monies. This is acutely true within church organizations. The cost of a fully developed Sunday School curriculum is about five times as much as the cost of ten years ago. The cost of paid staff for church organizations is about three times that of ten years ago. Building maintenance, utilities, insurance, etc., all reflect the same inflationary trend. Although the income of church organizations has increased, this increase is far below the increased expenditures. This disparity makes it imperative that church organizations make wise decisions concerning the distributions of available monies. Such informed decision making can best be enhanced by means of a solid evaluation process.

This is a large claim to put forth for the evaluation process. The question is naturally raised, can the process deliver the claimed results? For the past five years the author has been involved with church organizations ranging from the level of local parish to the national denominational agentry. The scope of this involvement has been varied from conflict resolution between pastor and congregation to a complete diagnostic study of the organization, its programs' personnel and purpose. In some of these efforts the process was stopped short of full evaluation, in these organizations there were very few constructive results. In other instances a full evaluation process was carried to completion, in these organizations constructive action was taken and respective goals were achieved. Whenever the evaluation process was totally employed, neither short circuited nor aborted, and when the evaluative results were used as the basis of informed decision making the consequent organizational changes and/or modifications resulted in more effective and efficient program planning and budgeting systems which led to more effective program results.

Evaluation is not a miracle drug to be given as a shot in the arm to church organizations. Evaluation is a well defined process of gathering and interpreting information appropriate to the decisions which are to be made concerning the organization. In a very real sense evaluation is a decision making process and when fully employed is successful because it allows the decision makers to have available the information necessary to make decisions.

The Meaning of Evaluation

Evaluation can mean different things to different people. So, before we go any further and become more confused we should look at a definition of evaluation which is the basis for this writing.

Evaluation is a data-gathering and interpretive process which provides the decision maker of any organization with information on 1) where the activity started, 2) why the activity was initiated, 3) where the activity was purposed to go, 4) what happened along the way, 5) where the activity actually arrived and, 6) what if any changes and modifications are needed to increase the effectiveness and/or efficiency of the activity.

This definition assumes that no activity is a total failure. Every activity has had a measure of impact upon the environment and all future activities can be built on the learning of what this impact has been. It is also an assumption contained within this definition and projected throughout this writing that the subject of evaluation is an activity or program. Persons are not appropriate subjects of evaluations rather their programmatic functions are. An evaluation might show the need for certain skills for task performance but it is left up to the decision maker of the organization to determine whether or not these skills are teachable or whether the program has need of the services of a person who has these skills from the outset.

More than a few leaders within church organizations have challenged the statment that persons are not appropriate subjects of evaluation. Their objections are buttressed with variations of the following explanations:

—the leaders are not businesslike
—the basic need is for better qualified persons
—the leaders do not set clear goals and clean objectives

All three objections miss the basic need of the church to offset the obstacles encountered on the way to high performance and results. They are at best half truths.

1. It is said again and again that if the church organization is to achieve high performance and desired results it must be run more businesslike. The church organization has problems with performance precisely because it is not a business. In church organization the word businesslike means, better control of the costs. In the name of efficiency many services essential to the fulfillment of a church organization's purpose are severely trimmed or halted completely. A balanced budget might be achieved but the intended effect, high performance, is seldom achieved.

When we look at successful businesses we discover they are characterized by a control of performance and results. Funds, even borrowed funds, are invested and risked to achieve performance and results. Efficiency is not ignored but it is not made a sacred altar to which all else must be subjugated.

It is effectiveness and not efficiency which is the greatest lack of church organization. Effectiveness cannot be gained by greater efficiency. Effectiveness comes as the result of informed decision making.

2. The cry for better people is one of long standing within church organizations. It has been believed that all church organizations would be healthy if only the leadership positions would be occupied by better qualified people.

Church organizations can, no more than businesses, pin their hopes on staffing every leadership position with iron men and geniuses. There are far too many positions to be filled. It is unreasonable to think that the people who do occupy leadership positions in church organizations are any less competent, any less honest or any less hard working than persons who occupy the corresponding roles in business. This is especially true within those denominations requiring seven or more years of higher education in order to meet the standards for leadership positions.

If the church organization cannot achieve high performance and desired results with men who only try hard, who are of normal and fairly low endowment, then these purposes cannot be achieved.

In recent years many persons who were

less than successful within church organizations have crossed over to accept managerial positions within businesses and are, in that environment, highly successful. The problems of church organizations are not the result of a lack of better people, nor can they be resolved by bringing in more qualified people. The fault is in the organization itself and not in the people.

3. The persons who adhere to the "better people" theory are also those people who tell us that church organizations will be healthy if the leaders are capable of setting clear goals and clean objectives.

Achievement is never possible except against clearly defined goals and along the paths of clean and specific objections. Only if targets are defined can resources be effectively allocated to achieve the organizations' purpose. This is true in church organizations as well as businesses. But the focal point to achieve effectiveness must be the definition of the purpose and mission of the church organization.

If the church organization has a clear statement of its purpose and mission, if the constituency believes this statement to be appropriate, and, if the programs which are being carried out are compatible with this statement then the church organization will be effective.

The purpose of evaluation is to ascertain whether all of the above conditions are alive and well within the organization. It is when we understand evaluation in this light that we say persons are not appropriate subjects of the process.

Resistance to Evaluation

Given this definition of evaluation, one must be questioning why more evaluation is not being done. Why, in fact, is it not required of all program efforts within every church organization? It seems ironic that when we are all bent on doing the best in every effort, and in order to do this we need all of the available information to help us make the most correct decision, we resist the very process which would enable us to answer that need. But, it is true, one of the biggest hurdles every evaluator faces is the resistance by organizational personnel to allow an evaluative process to be carried forth unimpeded.

It would be of help to any evaluator if we were to spend some time on thinking why this seemingly irrational resistance persists within church organizations.

It might be said that most evaluative efforts carried forth within church organizations have been little more than performance reviews. It also has been said that many evaluative efforts are no more than searching for evidence to validate decisions already made. These claims have an element of truth within them. But there are case studies which can point up the statistical facts supporting that seven out of ten church organizations which have been the subject of a thorough evaluation process have registered gains in the achievement of their stated goals. In these organizations stewardship has increased, participation at all levels of involvement has grown and a climate conducive to goal achievement, so necessary to church organizations, has been created and maintained.

Why are evaluative efforts resisted within church organizations? It is partly because of the organizational history. Evaluations have been ways to rid the organization of certain personnel. Evaluations have called for a change in organizational behavior and there are those who are fearful of any change. The history of church organizations has shown that an elite minority has been in control of making decisions and this elite minority fears that evaluative results will bring this control to light. Their fear of being found out and of losing control overrides their desire to have an effectively and efficiently run organization. There are also those people who have been sincerely dedicated in their efforts to keep a church organization operative. They have done the best they could. Any information which would point up deficiencies in their efforts would be interpreted by them as being judgmental. To this list of reasons any of you readers could add your own experiences. However adding to the list is not the major thrust of this book. We need to understand that there are reasons behind the efforts to resist an evaluative process. This understanding will enable the evaluator to gather a more complete set of useful data.

It is most important for the evaluator to set the tone, to create a climate that builds safety within the organizational structure if full cooperation in the evaluative effort is to be assumed. When an evaluator is asked to do an evaluation, every precaution should be taken in order to insure that the purpose of the evaluation is clearly stated and understandably known by all of the personnel affected by any decisions brought forth from the process.

Organizational resistance to the evaluation process also comes from the work completed by the evaluators. It is not uncommon for an evaluator, especially if the evaluator is a part of the organization, to use the process as an opportunity to put forth self-held solutions to the organizational problems. The feelings about the organization held by the evaluator should be carefully sorted out from the interpretation of the data gathered during the process. Most of us have our own understanding about the organizational structures and functions with which we come into contact daily. We know what we would do if we were in charge. If these preconceived ideas are not sorted out and kept in front of the evaluator at all times they will not only have a skewing effect upon the data interpretation but will also dictate the questions which are used to gather the information.

Understanding Program Activity

It has been stated earlier in this writing that the appropriate subject of an evaluation process is an activity or more precisely a program activity. In order to gain a clearer understanding of the evaluation process we ought to look for an understanding of what a program activity is.

Let's begin by comparing a program activity to an experimental research. In such research there is an occurrence, or occurrences of certain phenomena which we wish to understand in order that we might either control or cope with it. After having studied this phenomena occurrence we might imagine what would happen if we were to alter some of the environmental variables which are present at such occurrences. These imagined states we call scenarios. We then choose a scenario which we would like to bring about and begin to design an experiment which we believe will give us the desired results. Having described what is now happening and what we would like to see happen we ask the question: What actions do we take in order to bring about the desired change? The answer to this question is the experiment design.

Every program activity is started because of an existing condition which we would like to change, or the non-existence of a condition which we would like to have existing. The existing condition is the phenomena occurrences which we would like to control in one way or another. The hoped for condition is the envisioned scenario we would like to bring into existence. The strategy which we believe to be most successful in bringing about this change is the program activity. In experimental research the strategy is stated as a hypothesis. The hypothesis usually take the following form: If we bring such and such activities into being, then we can expect such and such a condition to exist. In programmatic terminology the scenario is usually called the program goal or goals and the strategy is referred to as objectives and ensuing steps. To put this in another way would be to say the existing condition is the starting point, the goal is our stated destination and the program activity is the route we plan to travel to arrive at our destination.

Most evaluations which are carried forth within church organizations only answer the question as to whether or not we have arrived at our predetermined destination. This kind of evaluative effort, if one would even call such effort an evaluation, is incomplete and not very helpful to organizational decision makers. A full evaluation process would inform the decision makers as to what happened from the discovery of the phenomena occurrences which we wanted to change through the present time. It would tell us what happened all along the way. It is therefore important that an evaluator work backward through the program from the present point in time through maintenance, implementation, planning, choosing and the conditions which existed at the beginning. It is only when all of this data is gathered and interpreted can we begin to make the most informed decision.

Types of Evaluation

This brings us to discuss the types of evaluation. Although there are more than one model of evaluation there are only two basic types of evaluative processes. There is that evaluative effort which is carried on while the program activity still remains alive; this type of evaluation is called **In Process Evaluation.** The second type of evaluative effort is that which is carried forth after the program activity has ceased; this type of evaluation is called **End Process Evaluation.** There is one other type of effort often referred to as being evaluative. This is the necessary research carried forth prior to implementing a program activity. The effort is one of making certain we are addressing the appropriate need. This effort is gathering data about programs which are presently going on or programs which had a similar goal as we presently envision them is only a diagnostic study and is only part of an evaluative effort as we shall see later on.

The **In Process Evaluation** and the **End Process Evaluation** both carry with them a unique set of problems for which the evaluator must constantly watch.

When an evaluation effort is initiated during a program activity the effort is an intervention into the program activity. It becomes one of the variables which impact the activity, program directors and program workers see a need to build coping mechanisms to render it innocuous to the successful achievement of the program. The program staff and director may feel their jobs are at stake and begin to function under more than the ordinary amount of stress. The validity of the data gathered by the evaluator will have to be checked more closely. The persons who are being questioned will attempt to give the *"right"* answers. Needed information which may be stored in records may be less than accessible to the evaluator.

An evaluative effort has an effect upon the recipients of the program as well. People will use the effort as an opportunity to give input in an attempt to get some individual need met. More often than not this unmet need has to do with gaining control. In one instance a local minister, who wanted to build up the Sunday School attendance, complained to the evaluator that the place of program distribution was not as accessible as it could be. He suggested that his church be the distribution center. He would use the program as bait to bring people to his church. If the evaluator had not completed a demographic study of the recipient population he could have been persuaded by the articulate argument of the pastor. It is also true that sometimes the success of a program activity could mean loss of power and/or prestige to other people within the target population and these persons will attempt to feed negative information to the evaluator.

An **End Process Evaluation** has its own unique set of problems in data gathering. The most obvious one is that of recapturing the accurate information about the program. Only part of the needed information would be found in written records. The rest of the data would have to be gathered by the recall method because it would be stored within the memories of the people involved in the program activity. Just as the environment is always changing while one is carrying on an **In Process Evaluation** so the environment undergoes changes from the time of the program activity to the time of the evaluative effort in an **End Process Evaluation.** This makes it more than a little difficult to reconstruct the activity as it was being carried forth.

Another problem with which the evaluator must cope in an **End Process Evaluation** is created by the possibility that the people who conceived and implemented the program activity are no longer with the sponsoring organization. This is especially true of church organizations where members come and go and paid staff are transferred or have quit their positions. If the program is such where the staff has been hired for the specific purpose of doing the activity, then the evaluator must try to find ways of reaching these persons.

Whether an **In Process Evaluation** is being carried forth or an **End Process Evaluation** is being completed it should be noted that the evaluation process will be effected by the daily activities of the organization. The gathering of data and the reliability of such data will be effected by personnel relationships which have been built during the organization's recent history. As in any organization so it is within many church organizations, feuds take time to be settled and debts are expected to be paid. Although the evaluator does not have the responsibility to resolve the feuds or bring about settlement of debts, he must so structure the methods of data gathering to insure a high degree of reliability. The evaluator must always be reminded that program activities do not exist in isolation from the total organizational activity.

What to Look For in Evaluation

We have talked a great deal about the data which an evaluator is to gather during an evaluative effort. We will be more specific as to just what kinds of information it is that the evaluator is looking for in later sections of this writing. But it would be helpful to us at this point if we could get hold of some general ideas as to what it is an evaluator would be looking for in the evaluation process.

An evaluator would want to know if the program activity would produce the same results in each situation to which it was applied. Another way of saying this is to ask whether or not the program activity had a direct causal relationship to the achieved results. Was it the planned recruitment and incorporation program of the local church which accounted for most of the increased membership or was it less responsible for the results than the fast growth of the population in the area? This information will tell us the impact of the program activity.

Another question of importance to the evaluator would be the one as to whether the coverage of the program activity was as broad as the initiators wished it to be. Was the program effective for the whole congregation or just for a segment? If the target population of the program was small in number would it be effective if it were expanded to a large number of cases? Would a goal setting process used with the governing body of the chuch be effective if it were expanded to include the total membership? This information would let the evaluator know what the coverage and the potential coverage of the program activity would be.

The evaluation process should also lay bare what set or sets of criteria were used in formulating and implementing the program activity. All of us are guided by a set of criteria, whether we are giving or receiving. These criteria are values which each of us has prioritized as guide in our own life. Did the program initiators take into consideration the values of the recipients? Were the value systems of the environmental culture wherein the program was carried forth considered? Were the values of the sponsoring organization considered? Some of the clear areas of program activities of the church organization in which values play a major role are Sunday School curricula selection, the distribution of benevolent funds, the role the organization plays in the changing and supporting of social systems.

The place of values in program planning plays a major role in the success of such programs.

The evaluator would also want to discover what kind and how much input the program sponsoring organization put into the program and what kind and how much benefit was actually received by the target population. This kind of information helps to define the amount of program attrition; how much of the available resources were used up in the program structure and how much went through the structure to the recipients. This is as true of services as it is of goods. If a person were hired to perform a certain function within the organization and if a disproportionate amount of his time were taken up in staff meetings and/or paper work the recipients of the service could be getting less than had been planned. Many times within church organizations a program director is provided with an office and a secretary when there is really little need for either. In these kinds of activities the resources are being inefficiently used.

In all aspects of the evaluative effort the evaluator should always ask the question as to just what facts would the decision maker need in order to make an informed decision as to continue the program as is or modified, abandon the program or duplicate the program activities. This is simply gathering the data which will enable the purpose of the evaluation to be reached.

The Determination of Useful Data

Throughout the evaluation process the evaluator will be gathering a large mass of information. There must be some guides as to what is important and useful data and what is extraneous material. There are four categories into which all useable data can be placed; *effort, effect, effectiveness areas,* and *efficiency.*

Effort is that which measures the quantity and quality of resources (money, materials, time and personnel) used in planning, initiating, and maintaining the program activity. Effect is that which measures the degree of impact the program has on the target population. It measures whether the effect was unitary or multiple, whether there were unintentional side-effects, how long the impact was influential upon the target population and whether that impact was cognitive, attitudinal or behavioral. Effectiveness areas define the parts of the total environment upon which the program had an impact. Efficiency defines whether or not a program works, why it works, and determines if there is any better way to achieve the same results. Efficiency is concerned with the evaluation of alternative paths or methods in terms of costs — *in money, time, personnel,* and *public convenience.*

All of the purposeful data will fit into one or more of these four categories. This does not mean that all other data should be discarded. It could very well be that some of the additional information which has been gathered would be of value to the organizational decision maker. This additional material should be collected separately from the evaluation report and given to the decision maker, labeled as additional information.

The Role of the Evaluator

The primary task of the evaluator is to gather information and present it in useable form enabling the decision maker to make the informed decisions which are required. While this process is being carried forth the evaluator must be aware that he, too, has a role in the organization. The evaluator's role must be compatible with the roles of other organizational personnel. He is in a sense sharing their turf; in some instances, such as the use of an outside consultant as the evaluator, he may be seen as violating the prescribed turf boundaries.

There are enough studies which have been made concerning leadership, its roles and power, to document how an outside consultant may often be seen as an unwanted and unauthorized person assuming leadership. It is up to the evaluator to make certain his role is understood by the personnel of the organization. The evaluator should make requests, not demands. He should also use the formal line of authority within the organization. If, for some reason, the evaluator feels the need to circumvent the formal line of authority he should present this problem to the client and request his help.

The evaluator must always be aware of his behavior and how it is being interpreted by the organizational personnel. In order to gain a thorough evaluation the evaluator depends to a large degree upon supportive cooperation from the people involved in the program activity. The evaluator's role is to create and maintain a climate in which this supportive cooperation can flourish. This climate creating should begin with the first meeting between the client and the evaluator. The evaluator should make the client aware of the interventions the evaluative process will likely bring about within the organization. Once the evaluator discovers where the needed information is stored he should be certain that all involved personnel be on board as to the need for the data, the use for such data gathered, and the full purpose of the evaluation should once again be made clear.

The evaluator is busy piecing out the whole program structure and function; as such, he does not perceive the program in the same way as do those people who are directly involved with the program. These people see individual worth and contribution more often than they see the worth and contribution of the total program. The evaluator should be aware of these persons' individual ego needs. As he records the aggregate statistics and observations, he could maintain the cooperative climate by sharing with the individuals observations about their contribution to the program activity. It is much easier to gather non-skewed data from within a friendly climate.

It would be well for the evaluator to remember that the stated purpose of his function is to evaluate the worth of a program. The people involved in that program believe in what they are doing and most likely believe they are doing a good job. These two points of view, that of the evaluator and that of the program people, are most conducive to conflict; the evaluator must do everything within his power to alleviate or at least diminish this source of conflict.

An evaluator might be involved in the change occurring within an organization, but he should not be the author of such change. He is there to: 1) determine the purpose of the evaluation, 2) gather the information which will be useful in achieving the purpose, and 3) present the information in useable form to the organizational decision maker.

Throughout this writing I have been speaking of the evaluator as if he were an outside party to the organization. This is not to be the case however with most evaluative efforts carried forth within church organizations.

The most frequently used method of choosing an evaluation for church organization is for the leadership to appoint a task force made up of member constituents and assign to them the task of evaluating program activities.

The concept of an internal evaluator raises the issue of the values carried by the person doing the evaluation. No evaluation can be a value-free process, whether the evaluator is an outside agent or an agent from within the organizational structure.

How does an evaluator keep proper perspective on information gathered and his own values? This question points up the most difficult balance required of all evaluators. There is a simple rule of thumb which will help a person to keep the proper balance. The evaluator should list his value assumptions which hold for the organization. This list should always be before the evaluator and whenever the interpretive process has been used the evaluator needs to ask what data document this interpretation. If such documentary data cannot be listed the evaluator should be cautioned that maybe his value assumptions have come into the picture.

It needs to be made clear that an evaluation requires a lot of work. Anyone who would agree to do an evaluation should be certain a large amount of effort will be expended before the evaluation process is completed. Throughout the process the evaluator will be faced with alternatives to doing a complete evaluation. If the goal of every evaluation is to enable an informed decision making process to be carried forth, then the evaluator should be committed to a process which will surface all available information. The information must be accurate and documented.

The process model detailed in the following chapters is a guide which when followed will help every evaluation to meet these two conditions of available and documented information.

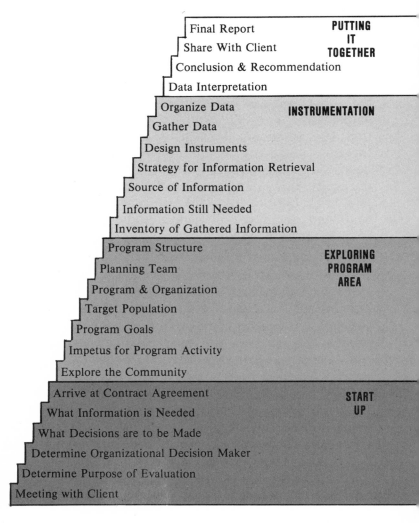

PUTTING IT TOGETHER
- Final Report
- Share With Client
- Conclusion & Recommendation
- Data Interpretation

INSTRUMENTATION
- Organize Data
- Gather Data
- Design Instruments
- Strategy for Information Retrieval
- Source of Information
- Information Still Needed
- Inventory of Gathered Information

EXPLORING PROGRAM AREA
- Program Structure
- Planning Team
- Program & Organization
- Target Population
- Program Goals
- Impetus for Program Activity
- Explore the Community

START UP
- Arrive at Contract Agreement
- What Information is Needed
- What Decisions are to be Made
- Determine Organizational Decision Maker
- Determine Purpose of Evaluation
- Meeting with Client

A PROCESS MODEL OF EVALUATION

Chapter II

A PROCESS MODEL OF EVALUATION

A model is a form which is to be used for comparison and guidance. A process model is a form which articulates the steps which should be taken in sequence in order to complete a defined process. The process model of evaluation which is described in the following pages has twenty-four steps which should be completed in any complete evaluation process.

It should be made clear that any process model is an ideal. If all conditions are perfect the model would fit on a one for one basis. But it is seldom the case that the organization and the organizational program activity are examples of perfect conditions. Therefore, the use of this model must carry with it the means for adaptation. The readers who will be involved in any evaluative process should become thoroughly familiar with the process and have a good understanding of why each step is included. This knowledge will enable modification of the process to fit the existing circumstances without aborting or distorting the effort of attaining the goals of a full evaluation.

Getting into an Evaluation Process

The first step of the evaluation process is the meeting between the client and the evaluator. This meeting is the springboard for the total process, therefore, the tone of this meeting should be one of clarity and honesty. Each of the participants should have a clear understanding of the other's position and expectations. The evaluator needs to be certain that the client knows what kinds of information to expect from the evaluation process.

At the first meeting with the client the evaluator should begin to keep a journal. This journal should be kept up to date throughout the complete evaluation process. At the end of the first meeting the journal should contain a clearly stated purpose of the evaluation, the name or names of the decision maker and the specific decisions needed to be made at the end of the evaluation.

Purpose of the Evaluation

The evaluation process is an intervention into the life of the organization. It makes demands on the organizational personnel which are different than the daily requirements they must meet. The evaluative process gathers data which carries information about people's efforts, capabilities and relationships. Such information could be damaging to program planners, directors and recipients. No evaluation should be done if the results are not to be used, and used for other than someone's personal agrandizement.

An evaluation process, when completed, should enable the leadership to move the total organization in a more harmonious manner. An effective program activity in which the goals are compatible with the overall goals of the organization will aid the organization to achieve its overall goal. The bottom line of any evaluation process should be the health of the total organization.

Many times an evaluation is asked for because the design of the program has included an evaluative step as condition for a supporting grant, an attempt to establish accountability, or simply because someone in an influential position has been informed that evaluation is good business. Often there has been no channel left open for the evaluative results to be fed back into the program activity's decision making process, or, as in the case of an End Process Evaluation, the feedback cycle cannot reach the organization's planning personnel.

An evaluation process is itself a program of the organization. As such there are needs which are to be satisfied, a scenario or hoped for results and a strategy for achieving these results. The purpose of an evaluation asks the question of what needs are to be satisfied. Is the information to be useful in planning a similar program? Are there decisions to be made concerning personnel, finances and/or location? Have difficulties developed in the program activity? Have certain side effects occurred? Is a progress report needed in order to request continuation of funds? These questions and others are those which will help to establish the purpose of an evaluation.

It is to be noted that here we are focusing on the purpose of the evaluation and not on the purpose of the program activity. The purpose of a program helps to determine the strategy of achieving the program goals. It is also true that the purpose of an evaluation helps determine the strategy in achieving the goals of such evaluation. The use of the evaluative data determines the form and function of an evaluation model. The purpose of an evaluation helps to determine what kind of information is needed, in which form the information is needed, when the information is needed and by whom the information is needed. We shall elaborate on these elements in the following pages but for now one needs to see the importance for a clear purpose to be stated. Any gathered data is subject to many forms of interpretation and if there is no purpose statement it would be coincidental if the interpreted data would be useful.

The Determination of the Decision Maker

Many times the author has discovered the people who ask for an evaluation are not the people with whom the responsibility of the program activity resides. This is not unusual. In many church organizations the governing body has the responsibility for monitoring all of the programs of the organization. This group will quite often ask for an evaluation. It could be argued these persons have the ultimate decision making within their purview. But it is true that in the majority of cases decisions concerning the programs of a church are left mostly in the hands of an appointed committee, for example, the Christian Education program. The governing body usually sets out the goals of the organization, however, the methods of goal achievement are usually left in the hands of committees or task forces with specific areas of responsibility assigned.

It is important for the governing body to be a part of the planning process for evaluation and in most cases will be the body who requests such an evaluation. It is equally important for the committee or task force who has the responsibility for the program activity to be evaluated to be a part of this process. It is the members of this latter group who are more apt to have knowledge about resources and who are closer to the target population of the program activity. Most important, these are the persons who will initiate action which may be indicated by the evaluation. They will also know the source of needed information as well as being the key links in making the needed information available.

It is true in most church organizations that an evaluator will be dealing with two levels of decision makers: those who determine policies and those who plan the strategies of policy implementation. Of course, as the evaluation process moves into data gathering the evaluator will have to make contact with all levels of decision making which are connected to the particular program activity to be evaluated.

When the decision maker has been determined the evaluator should take a second look at the stated purpose of the evaluation to ascertain if the purpose of the evaluation and the authority of the decision maker are compatible. If the information to be gathered and interpreted will not enable decision making within the purview of the client, then a second look needs to be taken at the purpose of the evaluation.

In the author's experience with church organizations it has been found that many of us have become experts in the fine art of making decisions for others. "The Sunday School teachers need more training," "The officers of the church need instruction in the Book of Church Order," "The Stewardship Committee needs to gain a better understanding of its task." These statements, the truth of each not denied, are attempts at making decisions for others.

What Decisions Are to Be Made

Having identified the person or persons who are responsible for making the decisions, then one who is thinking about doing an evaluation must decide what is the nature of the decision or the decisions to be made, what information is needed in order to make such a decision.

The evaluator needs to get a grasp of the decisions which are to be made. Are they decisions which affect strategies? Are they decisions which are wholly within the purview of the church organization? If not, what part of the decision belongs to the organization and what part belongs elsewhere?

It is at this point that the decision maker, and only the decision maker of the organization, can provide the answers and evaluate in what form the information should be presented to be useful in the pattern of decision making.

The time which has been set for the decisions to be made is very important to the evaluation, for evaluation processes require both work and time. Most evaluations demand that written material be perused, questionnaires be designed, tested and distributed, interviews be scheduled and held. These activities cannot all be accomplished at once. As we shall see later on in this paper, there is an appropriate sequence which is used in the data gathering process. The evaluator needs to have a time line of events in mind, and if there is not enough time allocated for a complete evaluation process to be carried out the evaluator should make clear to the decision makers just how much and of what quality information can be delivered at the required time.

Above all, the evaluator should not lead the decision maker to expect more information than can be delivered! The decision maker knows the responsibility and knows what information will be needed to carry out the responsibility. It is quite often the case that a time line can be extended in order to accomodate the complete data gathering process. But whatever the circumstances, the evaluator should know the decision with regard to the time line is not his, this decision resides with the organizational decision maker.

It is also important for the evaluator to know what organizational decisions are going to be made during the evaluation process. These necessary decisions could play a major role in the data gathering phase of the evaluation. If decisions are to be made which affect the organizational personnel, then the elements of skittishness and/or vindictiveness might be introduced. This might lead to skewed information to protect one's turf, to retaliate for not being chosen for a certain position, to square an old debt which has been harbored for some time, and other reasons.

The thought should not be fostered that these kinds of power conflicts do not happen within church organization. The staff of church programs may be voluntary but value systems and ego needs come into play in every aspect of every human life.

In summary, before the evaluator commits himself to an evaluative effort, certain information should be well in hand. This information should detail the purpose of the evaluation; it should identify the decision maker and the decisions which are to be made; and it is vital that the evaluator should also be aware of the climate of the organization.

If the evaluator is aware of what will be the ongoing decision making process during the evaluation, then the points of possible contention can be noted and special strategies can be readied for use. This awareness will enable the evaluator to be cognizant of the elements which might be needed to create and maintain a cooperative climate throughout the evaluation process.

Chapter III

SETTING THE CONTRACT

There may be some people who have total recall but most of us are not so gifted, so it is very important for the evaluator to keep complete notes. There will be many bits and pieces of information surfaced in the evaluation process and most of this information will have direct impact on data interpretation. Don't let any of the gathered material slip away.

The journal which has been kept during the first meeting with the client should be several pages of loosely organized notes. These notes will give the purpose of the evaluation, the name or names of the decision maker, the decisions which are to be made and the kinds of information the client feels to be necessary to enable an informed decision to be made.

Up to now the evaluator has asked questions of meaning and clarification. The client has asked questions about the evaluation process. The responses to this probing have been entered in the journal. These notes should now be put into manageable form.

The best way to accomplish this task, is by means of a written contract.

The Written Contract

It can be argued that a written contract is unnecessary. In most evaluation processes within a church organization the evaluator is from the inside of the organization. And in many instances the evaluation process is carried on by a volunteer or volunteer task group. It may be argued that the organizational personnel know and trust each other; the people have carried forth many tasks to their completion without a written contract. All of this may be true and if a contract was only a vehicle which declared the good faith of the client and the evaluator, then a written contract might not be necessary. However, a contract is more than a declaration of good faith signed by both parties.

A contract is a base line communication vehicle. A properly constructed contract will first serve as a check point to ascertain a common understanding by both parties of the purpose, focus, rationale and goal of the evaluation process. It is, in this sense, the first feedback loop built into the evaluation process. If there have been different interpretations given to the contents of the verbal agreement these differences will stand a better chance of being surfaced in a written document. It is advantageous to have any such misinterpretation surfaced and resolved at this preliminary stage of an evaluation than to be discovered farther along the evaluation process.

The differences which may be exposed can be looked at by both the client and the evaluator and in most cases can be reconciled. It may be that the purpose statement needs to be changed. For example, the purpose of an evaluation process might be stated: We wish to find out how effective the church newsletter is in communicating useful information about programs of the local church and the denomination. The evaluator has designed the evaluation process which would generate this information; how many persons read the paper, how much of the contents these same people can recall, what kinds of information are perceived by the readers to be most helpful, what part or parts are not read, etc. Upon reading the kinds of information the process will generate the client might respond that the real question needing to be answered is one of cost-effectiveness, comparing the paper with the bulletin inserts formerly used. This is an expansion of the original purpose statement and would require an additional unit for the evaluation process.

Another reason for a written contract is that such a contract will serve as a guide as the evaluator moves through the task. The statement of purpose and the area of focus will serve as norms for the preparation of the questionnaires and structured interviews. The time schedule will be set out in the contract with stated times for the evaluator to report progress to the client.

A written contract will also legitimize the cost of the evaluation. In the case of an outside evaluator the cost might be stated in one of several ways. The cost could be calculated as a total cost with the evaluator being responsible for the incurred expenses, or the cost could be stated as base price plus expenses. In some cases the cost is figured at price per hour plus expenses. This latter case is most rare primarily because most organizations would require a more precise figure as to total cost.

In the case of an evaluator from within the organization there should be two elements to the costing out of the evaluation costs. First, the commitment to pay for the expense of carrying forth the process and, secondly, there should be a written understanding for releasing the evaluator from normal organizational tasks in order that sufficient time be allowed for the evaluation process.

The Evaluation Proposal

There are several different forms which would be suitable to use to write a contract. The form which appears here is one that has been useful for the author. All contracts should have the type of information found in the following form.

Title: Proposal for the evaluation of the Pre-School Nursery run under the auspices of St. Paul's United Church. This proposal is made in response to a request made of Alan Drury by the Rev. Mr. Henry LeQuere.

Purpose:

The Central Conference has been asked to start a Pre-School Nursery in a neighboring parish. This evaluation is to surface information to aid in that decision making process.

Focus:

In the past the Central Conference has started Pre-School nurseries. These all have been set up using the same format. Some of these nurseries have been successful but three out of five have been less than satisfactory. This evaluation should surface information which would tell the conference if and why the nursery would be successful. There would also be evaluations of two other nurseries within the conference to enable the client to make comparative analyses.

Rationale:

Organizations, by their nature, are effected by their environments (the nature of their markets, the needs of their customers, and so on). As this environment changes the demands made on the organization change also. The level of income, the social class of the environment, the work pattern of the people all have an impact on the success or failure of program activities. It is good organizational practice to make a study of the total program profile before making a decision to replicate said program.

Desired
Results:

This study would yield information as to the demographic, economic and social status of the community in which the program is active. It would give a diagnostic analysis of program planning and maintenance which would show the effort, both quantity and quality, put forth. It will provide information as to the optimum conditions under which said programs might be duplicated.

Contract
Terms:

The evaluator will work with two people from the Conference who will introduce the evaluator and help provide him with access to records and personnel. The information will be gathered by means of observations (community), questionnaires and structured interviews.

The study will be completed thirty (30) days after an agreement has been made to award the contract. The time line for this evaluation is as follows:

Day 1
through 7:   The evaluator will explore the community, familiarize himself with the programs and with the organizations, read available records with reference to the programs.

Day 7:   Evaluator will meet with the client to share insights gathered from exploratory research and to check out any assumptions which might have been made from gathered data.

Day 8
through 21:   Evaluator will circulate question-naires and conduct interviews.

Day 21:   Evaluator will meet with the client to discuss non-respondents and to check to make sure no person inf-luential to the program has been overlooked in the data gathering process.

Day 22
through 29:   Evaluator will collate data and write out interpretation, formulate the recommendations.

Day 30:   Evaluator will give his written report to the client and will discuss report for the purpose of clarifica-tion. The client will determine if he has the needed information and in appropriate form to make the required decision.

Contract
Costs: The total cost of this evaluation will be fifteen hundred dollars ($1500.00) to be paid at the completion of the contract.

Signed: _____ Client
        _____ Evaluator
        _____ Date

If the evaluator is from within the organization the contract cost would make provisions for the expenses incurred by the evaluator to be paid for by the organization.

The above contract model is a form used for a short term evaluation process. It is adaptable for use when the evaluation process is to cover more than one program or a program broader in scope. When such is the case the evaluator would have to schedule more meetings with the client. The importance of these meetings cannot be overstated. The client should be involved in the evaluation process from the beginning to the end. Changes occur within the organizational environment and within the program environment. The evaluator and the client should be made aware of such changes and decide appropriate strategies to be used should modification of the process be indicated.

It can be expected that throughout the evaluation process circumstances will be different than those for which the process was planned. Such change in circumstances will call for change in the process of evaluation. For example, the time line may prove to be unrealistic, the information needed may be elsewhere than the source originally thought to contain it, which would require a different target population for the questionnaire and the interview schedule. For whatever reasons the need for modifying the process arises, the evaluator and the client need to make decisions together. A well written contract will allow for these decision making processes to happen.

When the client and evaluator agree that the fulfillment of the contract will provide the needed information to make the required decisions, the evaluator is free to begin to gather information.

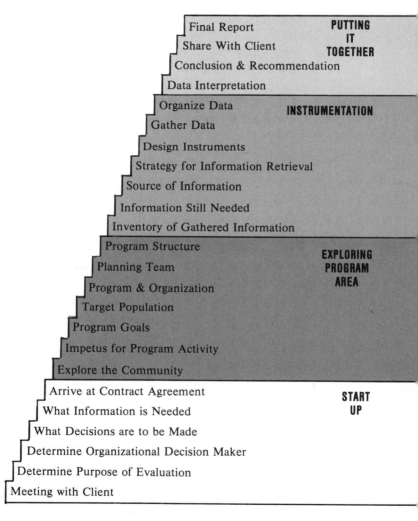

A PROCESS MODEL OF EVALUATION

Chapter IV

EXPLORATION OF
THE COMMUNITY

Before any research questions are asked or specific data gathered the evaluator should become familiarized with the organization sponsoring the program and the community in which the program activity is taking place. The evaluator should literally walk the geographical area of the organization and the program activity. The evaluator should make observation notes in the journal. These notes should be about the type of community: whether it is made up of light or heavy industry, shopping centers, residential or a combination of any of these. Is the residential area made up of apartments, condominiums, single family dwellings? What is the economical picture? Are the residents older couples, singles, young married adults, young families, etc.? Is there full employment or a high level of unemployment? The evaluator is constructing a community profile. Much of this information can be gathered from the Chamber of Commerce, State Employment Offices, Realtors, and Utility Companies.

There is no substitute adequate to provide profile information which will compare to first hand observation. As one walks through a community notes should be made on types of buildings under construction, kinds of merchandise being displayed and offered for sale, vacant lots, empty buildings, persons on the streets, upkeep or lack of upkeep of buildings. The evaluator should talk to local shopkeepers about the neighborhood. This information will help to construct a profile of the community as well as serve as an aid to interpret materials gathered from the Chamber of Commerce, etc.

The evaluator should be aware of the impact the sponsoring organization is having upon the community. What is the image of the organization held by the community? With many communities changing as rapidly as they are today, one should try to grasp the historical impact of the organization upon the community. It might very well be the case that a program activity is being effected because either the organization or the community is acting out of past expectations. If a neighborhood is in transition from being an upper middle-class community to a lower middle-class community and the church organization still gears program activities to the former population, community response can be something other than might be expected had the community remained static.

If the church organization has historically isolated itself from the social and political concerns of the community any new program effort by the organization reaching into these areas might be viewed with suspect. In such cases the organization would be best advised to first lay basic foundations in the social and political life of the community before launching a full-blown program activity. At least the organization must be made aware of the quantity and quality of the public relation work which must accompany any social or political oriented program.

After the evaluator has explored the community and has written the observation notes in the journal he can then begin to explore what gave impetus to the sponsoring organization for creating the particular program activity which is to be evaluated.

Determining the Impetus for the Program

Every program activity is started because of an existing need, whether that need is to create, alter or to eradicate a condition. The evaluator should discover what the basic need was which was the impetus for the organization to begin to think about the development of a program activity.

Sometimes this need is expressed in a straight forward manner, such as the need for an Adult Christian Education Class which has as its purpose that of aiding adults to become more knowledgeable of the Biblical literature. Other needs are not so visible. One church stated a need for a youth program to be established. The church hired a young person who was a Seminary student to be the youth director. The young man started and maintained an active youth program for a year. There were twenty youth of the church who were active in the program. The church officers were not satisfied and the young man became frustrated upon hearing this dissatisfaction being voiced. When the issue was surfaced it was discovered the church officers had expected a youth program would be effective in cutting down the incidents of vandalism occurring in the neighborhood. This need had never been expressed.

Another example of basic needs not being visible would be a stated need for a program of evangelism with the hidden need of raising more funds for the church being the true impetus.

The evaluator will have to probe to clearly define the need which was expected to be satisfied with the development and implementation of the program activity. The type of questions which will help discover the program impetus would be: What was going on in the organization or community which caused the program idea to be generated? What conditions existed which the organization wished to change?

Sometimes, the funds are made available if they are used for certain definite programs. At other times, especially with church organizations, the denominational agentry embarks upon a program which makes demands upon the local congregations or middle agencies. Such programs are cooperative efforts to help meet world hunger, establish mission posts, denominational fund raising efforts, etc.

When the evaluator is probing to discover the basic need he should also probe to discover who owns the need.

Who first made the need visible? who suggested this was an appropriate need for the organization to address itself to? Was it a need of the organization arising out of the environmental impact? Was it an internal need? These are the kinds of probing questions an evaluator should ask.

Whatever might be the results of this questioning the evaluator and the client should agree as to the basic need which served as the impetus to develop and maintain the program activity. This is useful information which will help the evaluator in comparing needs with program goals.

Journal — Organization's Image in Community

Shopkeeper: "Don't know much about that church. I guess they have services on Sunday but, of course, I don't live here so I can't say."

Resident: "They haven't seemed concerned about the neighborhood - most of their people don't live here."

Resident: "Since that new young preacher came there are a lot of older kids hanging around the church. That church has always been a part of this community. Of course, now-a-days not many people are interested in going to church - they're only out for a good time."

Banker: "They are doing a fine job. The scouts meet there and I think an AA group meets there, too. They give out food to people who need it, and they don't stick their noses into everyone's business."

Notes on my observations:

The church seems to be busy through the week. There are always 7 or 8 cars in the parking lot, buildings are well kept and programs are listed in the religion section of local newspaper.

The residential neighborhood around the church is made up mostly of people over 50 with few children at home - well kept, modest 2 apartment flats.

Population of Community:

20,500, 1975 bounded by route 6 on the north, Grand Avenue on the south, Oak Street on the west and Esenstadt Blvd. on the east.

Majority of residents in 2 apartment flats, quite a few garage apartments, 15 small apartment buildings (10-20 apartments per building).

Ethnic make-up:

52% Anglo, mainly from Appalachian mountain and Ohio River areas, 15% German, 21% Black Americans, 8% Italian Americans, 4% other.

Schools:

2 high schools, 2 junior high schools, 4 elementary schools, 1 private school (German Lutheran, 8 grades).

Mean Income: $7400

5 banks

7 finance offices

2 building, loan institutions

There are 47 taverns in the area.

Two industrial plants: Time Company (employs 3700 people) Fastener Manufacturer (washers, bolts, screws, etc. employs 1500 people).

Determining Program Goals

The evaluator should determine what the intended goals of the program activity are. It is far too idealistic to assume every program activity has clearly stated written goals. Even if this were the case, one should be aware that written goal statements can lend themselves to different interpretations made by different people. It is important to the evaluation process for the evaluator to know how the sponsoring organization, program planners and program directors understood the goals of the program activity.

It is often the case that sponsoring organizations may have viewed the program activity as a specific step in reaching a more general goal while the program planners and directors have viewed the program activity as being complete in and of itself. An example of such differing expectations held by involved parties would be a program activity of week long evangelistic meetings at the church. The policy making body of the organization might have viewed this as a source of potential new members. If this more general goal was not a part of the developer's or director's understanding, then the different parties would be using different criteria for measuring the success of the activity. It would also have demanded different strategy to have been employed in achieving the goal, such as follow-up calls, visitation and membership pitch.

It is more often the case than not that the goals of program activities are not written. They are instead implicit and assumed goals. The incidents of unwritten program goals for church organizations are somewhat diminishing at the present time but the number is still very high.

Implicit goals are difficult to ascertain and require more probing efforts by the evaluator. Partially, this is true because these goals are stored in peoples' heads and recall is always more vague than that information gathered from written documents. Another reason resides in the fact that many persons who are involved in a program activity have the need to justify what has taken place. Therefore, some will have changed the earlier understanding of the goal to reflect the present output of the program activity.

An evaluator needs tools to sort out what the original goal of the program was from what the present goal might be, if they are different. Such questions as: What did you envision happening or not happening in order to consider this program activity successful? Where do you now see the program activity leading? What was the scenario envisioned which when brought into being would have eliminated the need to which this activity addressed itself?

This sorting out of prior held goals and presently held goals, if they are different, need not be considered as judgmental or as a mark of program failure. It might very well be if the presently held goals are achieved they are of more value to the organization than the original goals. The evaluator is only to report out the difference if any exists. The client makes the decision as to the worth of the goal achievement. Again the caution should be heeded by the evaluator to be certain his values are separated from the information as it is gathered and reported out to the client.

There are times when a program activity which is to be evaluated has been an on-going program of long duration when the distance in time from the beginning to the present is so great that few if any persons remember any goals and few remain who were in the program from the beginning. It would be next to impossible to surface the original goals and in all probability the organization and community would have changed to the degree of making these goals inappropriate. In such instances the evaluator could at best complete a diagnostic study which would surface what is presently occurring, what needs are being met, and at what cost the program is operating. There are many documentations which claim the worth of such studies and a well-trained evaluator could do the diagnostic study most adequately.

When the evaluator has determined the goal or goals of the program activity and there is a common interpretation of these goals held by the evaluator, client and program planners, then one needs to look for and identify the intended recipients of said activity.

Determining the Target Population

The beneficiaries or recipients of the program activity's out-put are commonly referred to collectively as the target population. The evaluator wants to know whether this population is contained within the organization's membership. If the program activity is meant to benefit those people within the organization, the evaluator will know what to look for when he studies the planning process used for this program activity. Who was involved in the decision making process, who was excluded, from whom did the planners seek information, etc., these are important to an evaluation process. The same reasoning holds for a program activity whose target population resides outside the organization's membership. It is often the case that program activities are decisions made for other people. Even though the intent of the decision is to favorably serve others, it is still common knowledge most people desire to have a part in decision making processes which affect their lives. Persons may not be resisting a program activity because it is less than helpful; they may be reacting to their exclusion from the planning process. This type of information, whether or not members of the target population were in on the planning stages of the program activity, will help the evaluator measure the effect and the effectiveness areas of the program.

Much of the literature coming out of the management science discipline speaks of open systems, feedback cycles, organizational development, etc. These terms are all ways of describing the importance of involved personnel of organizations having access to give input to the decision making processes. These different management styles are put forth in recognition of the importance of enhanced human contribution in an effort to attain more and better output for the same input. If these methods are successful, and their wide use in the business world speaks to at least a measure of success, then the lack of these methods in a church organization would certainly have an effect upon the success of any program activity.

More will be said along this line when the profile of the program planning team is discussed. But for now the importance of determining the intended target population should be clear.

Chapter V

THE PROGRAM AND
THE ORGANIZATION

The evaluator should now have a fair understanding of the external framework in which the program activity is to function. The main thrust and focus of the activity should be known. What remains to be explored is the organizational framework of which the program activity is a part and the structure of the program itself.

It is about at this point in the reading when the reader will begin to question if all of this preliminary legwork is important or even necessary. Many will be wondering just when we are going to get to the evaluation process, when we start interviewing, sending out questionnaires, and begin to get some hard data. The information gathering has already begun. The journal notes made from your observations, readings, etc., will be valuable information which serves to construct appropriate questionnaires and interviews; it will help decide who has what kind of information; and the information gathered about the community, the organizational territory, can be checked out with the client to see if there exists a common understanding. It is not uncommon for a client to be so involved in the organizational activity he will not have noticed a change in the community. Unless there has been a recent occasion for the organization's degree of influence to be tested, the client may not be aware of any change which might have taken place. The program activity might have been launched under an erroneous assumption about organizational influence which could have a bearing on the success or failure of such activity.

The evaluator should now begin to determine where the program to be evaluated fits into the organizational picture. Seldom is there an organization which has only one program activity. The intraorganizational relationship of the different programs has a strong bearing on the functioning of each program. Most program activities are not isolates, especially in church organizations where you can find two or more programs related by committee structure, budget item, and in some cases competing for the same resources as well as aiming for the same target population.

It is important for the evaluator to determine where the particular program activity touches other program units of the organization. Are there overlapping goals, where two programs are separately working to bring about the same results? How are priorities of the organization listed? Is the program to be evaluated high or low on the priority list? Is the program one which fits into the traditional programming area of the organization? Is it a program which is experimental in character? Does it seek to serve in a controversial way?

Figure 5.1 illustrates that although the evaluator does set the program activity apart from other activities of the organization in order to study it more completely he must also study the activity as it relates to the other programs within the organization.

The evaluator should get an organization chart and make note of the lines of authority and communications. Where does the program activity fit on such a chart? Is the authority clearly defined or vague? Are programmatic decisions made by one part of the organization and budgetary decisions made by another part? Are there built-in communications channels allowing for program managers and budget managers to have an interface?

One of the basic thrusts of the evaluator's exploring the organization matrix is to discover those points where less than full ownership of the program activity might occur, the points where competitive effort is built into the organization. Is the competition for scarce financial resources, manpower resources, space resources, etc.?

Where no organizational chart exists the evaluator should, together with the client, construct such a chart. This can be done through use of by-laws, constitutions, job descriptions, and existing behavior patterns.

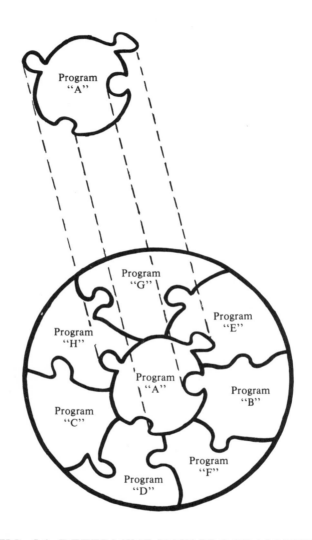

FIG. 5.1 DETERMINE HOW PROGRAM FITS
INTO TOTAL ORGANIZATION

Figure 5.2 illustrates a simple organizational chart and a listing of committee responsibilities. From this basic chart it is not hard to imagine programs which might overlap two or more committees' areas of responsibility.

The Make-up of the Planning Team

It has been stated in the first chapter that an evaluator must have an understanding of what a program activity is. The evaluator will need to reconstruct the program activity from its beginning until the present, whether it is an "In Process Evaluation" or an "End Process Evaluation." By now the purpose, need to be satisfied, goals and target population of the program activity, have been determined. The information which is needed to complete the program profile is that which tells about the planning team, the start-up strategy and the organizational structure of the program activity.

Who were the members of the planning team who brought the program activity into existence? Were outside people brought in or were people from the organization brought together for this task? Were any people from the target population members of the planning team?

The evaluator needs to discover what processes were used to mold these persons into a team. Was an outside consultant involved in the planning? Sometimes organizations can bring people from within who have the needed skills

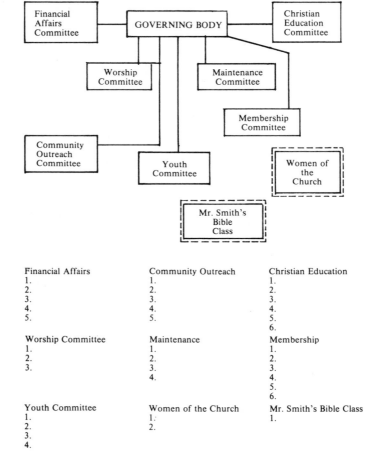

Financial Affairs
1.
2.
3.
4.
5.

Community Outreach
1.
2.
3.
4.
5.

Christian Education
1.
2.
3.
4.
5.
6.

Worship Committee
1.
2.
3.

Maintenance
1.
2.
3.
4.

Membership
1.
2.
3.
4.
5.
6.

Youth Committee
1.
2.
3.
4.

Women of the Church
1.
2.

Mr. Smith's Bible Class
1.

FIG. 5.2 ORGANIZATIONAL CHART AND COMMITTEE RESPONSIBILITIES

for the task. At other times the needed skills are those which can be learned in short training sessions. It should be determined which course of choosing the personnel has taken.

Another bit of information that would be useful when developing the planning team profile is whether or not the members of the team had other responsibilities. At times when people have more than the ordinary work load some duties get short-circuited. In the case of planning a program activity the planners might short-cut the planning and implementing process which would have an affect upon the activity; or they might be neglecting their regular organizational tasks which could cause hard feelings to be harbored against the planned program activity.

The evaluator should also gather data concerning the amount and quality of research carried forth by the planning team in putting the program activity together. When a organization is attempting to market either a product or a service the chances for success are greatly enhanced by a thorough study of the market. Many programs of church organizations have been less than successful because the potential market, or target population, had not been surveyed. A highly successful program for recruiting new members in an area with a rapidly rising middle income population cannot be assumed to be successful in an area which is just as rapidly becoming a low income section of the community. Fund raising programs which are successful in upper middle income sections of the community might not be as successful in areas with low income and a high unemployment rate.

Most church organizations, expecially those in non metropolitan areas and transitional areas, are usually faced with the challenge of planning program activities for target populations with mixed financial and social strata.

The evaluator needs to discover if the planning team took seriously the characteristics of the community in their planning process.

If the program was of an educational nature what amount of research was done concerning the available materials, both for the content of the program and the methods of presentation? Did the planners study other programs which were similar? Were several alternatives to the chosen plan studied?

The evaluator should check out the documentation for the choices made. Again, this is not a matter of being judgmental; it is an attempt to discover what effort went into the planning processes and to get an idea as to what modifications, if any, should take place if the program is to be continued or replicated.

The Organizational Structure of the Program

How was the structure for the start-up, maintenance and delivery of the program set up? Most program structures have three basic levels of decision making: the manager, whose responsibility is that of keeping all program units tied together by creating lines of authority and communications; the program directors, whose responsibilities are those of making strategy and production compatible with one another, the program implementors, whose major responsibility is that of distribution. In many program activities of church organizations these three decision making processes are vested in one or two persons. But in all cases the structure should enable the strategy to function. The line of authority should allow the decision making processes at each program level to function smoothly. At points where there are unpredicted interventions — those occurrences which do not follow the expected patterns — communications channels should be such to allow for fast alterations to be made and implemented. Every program activity should be structured for flexibility.

It is useful for the evaluator to explore whether or not the lines of authority and communication were formalized, that is written down, in a procedure manual. A good way to check for the adequacy of such written material is for the evaluator to imagine some irregularity occuring in the program, then to check the manual to see if he can trace the path that the needed communications would have to follow. This is checking for what feedback cycles, if any, were built into the operation procedures.

The evaluator should also seek out information concerning the training given to program people. Was there any training offered, if not, was this a conscious decision? Was there an effort made to build a working team of the people chosen to implement the program activity? These are important questions asked to discover the effort which went into the start-up of the program.

Another piece to this information puzzle deals with publicizing the program activity. Many program activities have failed in delivering the expected results because the public relations effort was much less than the situation demanded. It is a simple case of making decisions without first gathering the available and pertinent information, such information, for instance, as offering the programs on dates which are accessible to the target population. The checking out of possible locations for distribution points is also a must in a well planned program activity. Many times the advanced notice of the program activity and the program's starting date are literally on top of each other. How were the announcements of the program activity made? What forms of media were used? What was the pattern of distribution of the announcement? All of this information is of value when evaluating the effort put into the start-up strategy of a program activity.

When the evaluator has completed the first eleven steps of the evaluation process another meeting with the client should be scheduled. This meeting is for clarification of material gathered, and to see if the client has any additional input or some useful interpretation of the data in hand.

The financial records of the program activity should be studied and the records compared with the information which has been gathered concerning the actual tasks attempted and accomplished from program idea to program implementation. Were the tasks to be performed provided for in the budget? Were there any tasks for which a budget was supplied and not carried out? Why? The information being sought is the amount of financial effort put into the start-up of the program activity.

There are times when the total dollar amount budgeted for program start-up would seem adequate but some task needed to get the program activity rolling was not performed. This could come about because the budget line items were too restrictive. There was no flexibility allowing for adjustments to be made. This is most often the case when the program activity is a completely new venture for the organization. When the program activity is new there are few, if any, models to serve as guidelines for funding the operation. It is in such instances the program planners and implementors need discretionary powers to adjust the budget within prescribed limits.

Perhaps an illustration would best describe this point of program planning. A regional body of a church organization initiated a program which would meet the need of sharing resources among five districts in a more effective and efficient way. The program and budget was approved by the regional body. Enabling funds were provided for the employment of a program director, office, secretarial help and travel. As the director became involved in the process it was discovered that training sessions would be needed to establish the program. Although the regional body had considered this action they had not provided funds for its happening, reasoning that they had employed a person who was skilled in the area and would do the training as part of his task. What was not considered and provided for was the cost of bringing people together for training events. The director of the program had to ask for discretionary powers to adjust the budget. Even though these powers were granted the program activity fell three months behind the schedule for program completion. This proved to be a costly oversight in program planning.

As in all areas of evaluation, the evaluator is to be alert for how the unexpected events were encountered and dealt with. The question needs to be asked whether or not better planning would have more effectively and efficiently accounted for the unexpected.

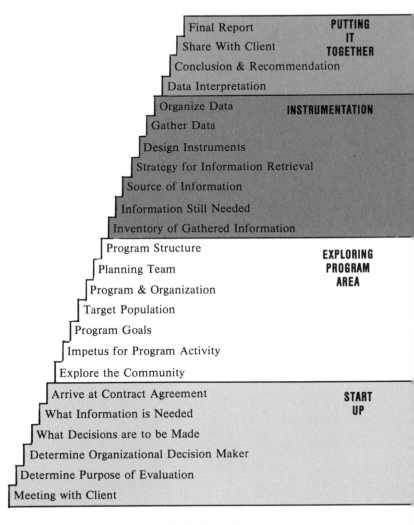

Final Report

Share With Client

PUTTING IT TOGETHER

Conclusion & Recommendation

Data Interpretation

Organize Data

INSTRUMENTATION

Gather Data

Design Instruments

Strategy for Information Retrieval

Source of Information

Information Still Needed

Inventory of Gathered Information

Program Structure

EXPLORING PROGRAM AREA

Planning Team

Program & Organization

Target Population

Program Goals

Impetus for Program Activity

Explore the Community

Arrive at Contract Agreement

START UP

What Information is Needed

What Decisions are to be Made

Determine Organizational Decision Maker

Determine Purpose of Evaluation

Meeting with Client

A PROCESS MODEL OF EVALUATION

Chapter VI

INVENTORY OF GATHERED INFORMATION

At this point in the evaluation process the journal is full of information. The information has been gathered by observation, reading records and documents, and in discussions with the client. There is still more information needed for a complete evaluation process to be accomplished. Most of the needed information will have to be gathered by the use of questionnaires and specific structured interviews. Before the instrument can be prepared, some means should be used to sort out the information in hand and to make clear what information is still needed.

Figure 6.1 is a simple chart which will aid in sorting out the gathered information and to determine what additional information is still to be gathered. If the proposal for evaluation is adequately written and the journal has been kept up throughout the process, all of the information needed to fill out the top half of this chart will be readily available.

INFORMATION GATHERED			
EFFORT	EFFECT	EFFECTIVENESS AREA	EFFICIENCY
Purpose Needs Goals Program Planning Organizational Structures Publicizing Training of Program Personnel Make-up of Planning Team	Needs-Whose? Goals — Beneficials? Public Relations Accessibility of Program Output Priority Given to Program Make-up of Planning Team	Target Population Study of Community Intended Direction of Program Program Goals	Adequate Budget? Program Flexibility Completeness of Program Planning Alternatives Explored and Considered

INFORMATION STILL NEEDED			
EFFORT	EFFECT	EFFECTIVENESS AREA	EFFICIENCY
Operation of Program Location of Delivery Point	Input vs. Output Original need being eliminated or diminished?	No. of Beneficiaries Reaching People other than Target Population Location of Delivery Point	Staff number of workload Cost of Input vs. Worth of Output

FIG. 6.1

The sample chart shows the kinds of information gathered and the appropriate categories under which this information falls. It will be noticed some kinds of information fall under more than one category. The sample chart illustrates general kinds of information. When the chart is being filled and during an actual evaluation process, specific information needs to be inserted. For example, under "needs" specific details as to actual statements concerning, "what?" "how discovered?" "whose needs?", etc. should be written in. Properly prepared this chart will help in reporting out the findings of the evaluation process.

Most of the needed information will have to do with program delivery. It has, for the most part, been determined what the organization has put into the program, such as planning, team selection, training, publicizing, studies, etc. The evaluator will now determine what kinds of information is still to be collected, the source of this information and the ways by which it is to be retrieved.

Who Has Needed Information

By studying the program structure an idea of what one would expect to find happening in program maintenance should be formed. Is program operations overstaffed? How is the workload distributed? What is the rate of converting input to output — how many dollars does it cost to deliver how much service or product?

A study of the target population is needed. How do the recipients see the program output? Have their needs been met? If not, why? What benefits does the target population perceive as a net gain? If the program were to be continued what modifications would the target population suggest?

The people within the community other than the target population can provide the information about added benefits from program activity. The target population and others can give information about adverse side effects of the program activity.

Some of this information can be gathered from the program activity records. Access to these records should be assured. The client is the person who can give this permission.

The evaluator should make a list of the information which needs to be gathered. The bottom part of the chart as illustrated in Figure 6.1 is a convenient way of listing the needed information. It can be categorized in the four areas as shown. As is true in the categorization of information already gathered some kinds of information will be useful in more than one category. For example, "input vs. output" will be useful in measuring both effect and efficiency.

The determination of where the different kinds of information is stored can be mapped out on the same chart. A simple coding will aid in the process, such as "T.P." for target population, "C" for community, etc. How the information is stored can also be listed on the same chart, such as written reports, newspapers, in people's heads, etc. The questions to ask to decide how the information is stored are: Is it accessible to be read? Is it in record form? Are there tapes of the meetings? Are there well-kept minutes of all proceedings? Is the information in the minds of the participants, program people or clients?

There is a word of caution to the evaluator concerning information which is in written form. If the written material is a description of what is happening in the program operation, then the evaluator needs to design questions which will serve to verify if the actual happenings were as described in the records. There can be discrepancies between what is reported in progress reports and what is going on in the field. Just as an evaluation process should be reported out with documentation for conclusions made, so progress reports should have accompanying documentation. Where such documentation is lacking the task of the evaluator is to dig it out. Remember, an evaluation process describes what happened all during the program activity's existence.

How to Retrieve Needed Information

At this point in the evaluation process the evaluator needs to meet with the client. The client should be told what information has been gathered and what information still needs to be retrieved. Most decision makers are on top of the organizational activity. They are the best source to verify who has what information and in what form the information is stored. They are also the persons who can authorize any release of information which might be needed.

Figure 6.2 illustrates a simple chart which can serve as a guide to the rest of the evaluation process.

INFORMATION NEEDED	WHY IT IS NEEDED	SOURCE OF INFORMATION	HOW IT IS STORED	HOW TO RETRIEVE INFORMATION
How much of program out-put was received by target population	To measure effect, efficiency, effective-ness area	Target Population	Memory	Interview

FIG. 6.2

In any given evaluation process there is probably no single way which will retrieve all necessary information. Even if all of the information is stored in written form there is still the need to ask questions which will serve to validate the written material. The question which plagues most evaluators is when to gather data by means of a mailed questionnaire and when to use structured interview schedules. There are no simple solutions to this problem but there are guides which will help the evaluator to decide the most appropriate means of retrieving information. The evaluator should consider the advantages and disadvantages of both the questionnaire and the interview. If the advantages override the disadvantages and if the advantages of one means out-weigh the advantages of the other, then that par-ticular means of information retrieval should be used.

Space does not permit a thorough investigation of the advantages and disadvantages of the mailed questionnaire and the structured interview schedule. Only the more obvious state-ments about the use of both will be stated here. The reader is encouraged to search out more detailed information from available writings.

The mailed questionnaire allows for the maximum coverage for the minimum expense both in time and money; allows for a wider geographic contact; reaches people who are unavailable for interviews; allows for the respon-dent to give more consideration to the answers; allows for greater consistency in the manner in which questions are asked and diminishes the intervening impact of the interviewer.

The greatest disadvantage in using the mailed questionnaire is that of non-returns. Peo-ple will respond to short, precise and pertinent questionnaires more readily than to longer ones, but there is the possibility of misinterpretation of the questions asked, and there is no follow-up which would allow for clarification.

The structured interview schedule allows for a face to face contact between the interviewer and the subject, usually within the more comfor-table arena of the subject's home territory. The interview is also conducted at the subject's con-venience both in time and place. The yield of useable returns is very high, for most people are willing to cooperate and any misinterpretation can be clarified during the course of the interview. The answers are usually more spontaneous as the subject does not have time to give what he or she thinks are the expected answers. Also, group discussions can be held with personal interviews. This can be advantageous if the information to be gathered calls for recall by the subject; group members can trigger the memories of one another with individual responses.

The major weakness of the structured interview schedule is the cost in time and money. There is also the problem of finding compatible time schedules for contact between the interviewer and the subject to take place. The skills required to be used on personal interviews are such that unless the interviewer is trained and competent in this area the information recorded may be inaccurate and incomplete. Finally, the time allotted for most interviews is always cut short. There should be enough time allocated for the subject to respond at his or her own pace.

The evaluator will have to make the final decision whether to use mailed questionnaires or the structured interview schedule. It has been the author's experience that in evaluation processes of church organizations' program activities it is necessary to use both. The rule of thumb which is most easily followed is when time and cost permit and if the subjects are accessible, use the structured interview schedule.

Designing and Testing Data- Gathering Instruments

Before instruments can be designed a thorough grasp of the arena to be studied, a clear understanding of the objectives of the evaluation and a knowledge of the information needed should be had. Economy and efficiency are important criteria. The instruments should surface the data needed but not more.

There are basic rules for designing instruments. The language should be comprehensible to the target population. The words used should have clear and precise meaning, offering the least chance for error in understanding. Avoid long questions; the longer the question the more chance there is for ambiguity and confusion. Above all, neither the questionnaire nor the interview should be an affront to the subject. The evaluator should make it as easy as possible for the subject to respond.

There is no simple way to construct a questionnaire or an interview schedule. Help can be obtained by studying questionnaires which others have used. In most cases every evaluative effort will require instruments which are specifically designed for the task at hand. The example for building questions which follows should be used as a guide. Again, the reader is encouraged to seek out books written on the subject of designing instruments for data gathering.

A simple design which is useful in designing questions is one which is divided into four parts:

1. What information is needed.
2. The source of the information.
3. The indicators of the information.
4. The questions which will produce the information.

The information which is needed can be stated as: How much of the input to the program was received by the intended beneficiaries? The issues of this question are, first, the attrition, and, secondly, the actual benefit. The source of this information is divided. The amount of input would be known by the program planners and the amount of benefits received would be known by the target population. The indicators of this information would be dollars and goods invested in the program and the amount of goods received. There would need to be two sets of questions, one directed to the program planners and the other directed to the target population.

The questions which would be put to the program planners would be fairly easy to formulate. Information about total budget and about cost of program maintenance could be gathered by direct questioning. However, it would be more difficult to get a comparable figure for the evaluative purposes. If the product were such as food or clothing, there could be a cost accounting process which would produce a dollar figure. When the program output is a service such as drug counseling, legal advice, educational, etc., there would be no simple way to arrive at a comparable cost figure. In the latter case the evaluator could use as indicators the number of different persons who received the services and the number of times each person was served. The questions used would be simple and direct. If the program records are the source for number of persons served, the evaluator should sample the target population in order to validate the program records.

The questions asked of the target population would differ slightly from those asked of the program planners. The information needed from the recipients is that concerning perceived worth of benefits received. Such questions as: What is now happening which would not be happening if the program were discontinued? How were these needs met before this program was offered? If you could alter this program in any way what changes would you make? How often do you participate in these programs? Has the frequency of participation changed over the past few months? Which way, more now or less?

The specificity of these questions would have to be dictated by the kind of program activity being evaluated.

Questions to be used in a structured interview schedule are generated in the same fashion as those questions used in a mailed questionnaire. The questionnaire would have two or three questions for each indicator; the interview would have one question with directional probes to sharpen the focus of gathered information.

A simple schematic form illustrating the question building process is presented in figure 6.3.

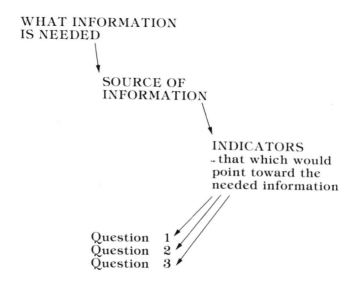

FIG. 6.3

After the questionnaire and interview schedules have been designed and built, the next step is to test these instruments to ascertain if the information they produce is the needed information.

Testing the Instruments

There are several good reasons for testing the data gathering instrument prior to general use. Language is always a problem. The evaluator knows what he means when certain words are used but he cannot be certain the same meanings will be given those words by others. The questionnaires and interview schedules are designed to surface specific information. Many times questionnaires fall short of producing the specificity of information desired. When this happens the evaluator must either go back to the target population for more information or complete the process with less information than could be available. It is safer to pretest.

Also, persons who respond to data gathering instruments are giving of their time and energy. The evaluator should not be so thoughtless as to ask the respondents to give of themselves in this way by filling out questionnaires which have been carelessly constructed.

In order to check out the effectiveness of the data gathering instruments the evaluator should choose a few persons from the population of those who will be questioned. These selected persons should be accessible for face to face contact. The questionnaire and the interview schedule should be administered and time allotted to allow the evaluator to question the sample population about areas of clarity, vagueness and meaning of the instrument used.

The evaluator will then collate this information and present it to the client. Together, the client and the evaluator will study the test results to determine if the information gathered is useable for decision making purposes. If, however, the client says more information is needed or different information is needed then the evaluator, along with the client, will determine how best to rework the instruments to acquire the needed information. If the information is found to be adequate the distribution of the questionnaire and the scheduling of interviews can be set into motion.

Gathering the Data

The rule of thumb for any data gathering effort is to make it easy for the subject to respond. A self-addressed stamped envelope should be included with each mailed questionnaire. All structured interviews should be conducted at the convenience of the subjects and should always be set up with an appointment.

A covering letter which details the purpose and the goal of the evaluation as well as the authority for the evaluator to gather the information should be sent out to all intended subjects and should be signed by the client. There should be a date set for the expected return of the questionnaires. This data should be carefully planned, the subject needs adequate time to work it into his or her schedule, but it should not be set so far in the future that the subject is apt to postpone responding and forget it.

All communications mailed to the subjects should be typed and in a form easily understood. It is good to write a sentence or two of introduction to each section of the questionnaire which would help the subject understand the kinds of information being asked for. The best advice is to treat the subject as if you were the respondent.

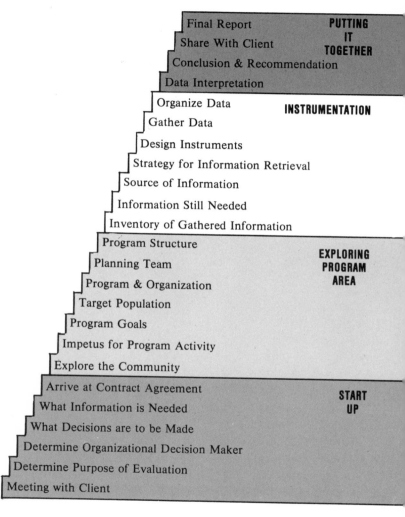

Final Report
Share With Client
Conclusion & Recommendation
Data Interpretation

PUTTING IT TOGETHER

Organize Data
Gather Data
Design Instruments
Strategy for Information Retrieval
Source of Information
Information Still Needed
Inventory of Gathered Information

INSTRUMENTATION

Program Structure
Planning Team
Program & Organization
Target Population
Program Goals
Impetus for Program Activity
Explore the Community

EXPLORING PROGRAM AREA

Arrive at Contract Agreement
What Information is Needed
What Decisions are to be Made
Determine Organizational Decision Maker
Determine Purpose of Evaluation
Meeting with Client

START UP

A PROCESS MODEL OF EVALUATION

Chapter VII

ORGANIZING GATHERED INFORMATION

When the interviews have been completed and the questionnaires have been returned this information must then be put into some organized form to aid in the interpretation. The way the information is organized will be determined by the evaluation model which has been used, but some general principles can be given to serve as a guide for the evaluator. The guidelines which follow comprise the pattern used by the author.

1. List information gathered during exploration of community; categorize this material as it answers questions about effort, effect, effectiveness areas and efficiency.
2. List information gathered which describes the sponsoring organization; use the same four categories in classifying this material.
3. List information gathered from the program activity which describes the processes of planning, developing, starting and maintaining the program.

Categorize in the same way as above.

4. List the information gathered by means of the model questionnaires and structured interviews. Use the general headings of community, organization, program activity and target population, subdividing into the sub-categories of effort, effect, effectiveness areas and efficiency.

5. Combine these four lists into one form which contains all of the information useful to the evaluation.

6. Make notes of gathered information which might be extraneous to the evaluation but could be useful information for the organization.

The form which now contains the gathered information would have the following appearance:

COMMUNITY

EFFORT	EFFECT	EFFECTIVENESS AREAS	EFFICIENCY

ORGANIZATION

EFFORT	EFFECT	EFFECTIVENESS AREAS	EFFICIENCY

PROGRAM ACTIVITY

EFFORT	EFFECT	EFFECTIVENESS AREAS	EFFICIENCY

TARGET POPULATION

EFFORT	EFFECT	EFFECTIVENESS AREAS	EFFICIENCY

FIG. 7.1

If the questionnaires and interview schedules were built with the help of Figure 6.1 there should be few problems in collating the gathered data and transferring them to the above chart (Figure 7.1).

Once the information is categorized the evaluator studies the chart and begins the interpretation process.

Interpreting the Information

Now that the information has been gathered and categorized the question for the evaluator is: What does it tell about the program activity? It can be recalled at the beginning of this process the evaluator and the client met. At that meeting they raised the questions, What is the purpose of the evaluation? What decisions are to be made? and, What information does the client need in order to make these decisions?

These were the questions whose answers guided the data gathering processes and they will continue to serve the evaluator as guides to interpreting the gathered data. If the purpose was to find out if there were more efficient ways to continue an on-going program the evaluator would be searching the data for information about costs in time and money, possible points of waste, amount of attrition, etc. Of course, the more obvious points about cost are those directly connected to dollars, but the gathered information can yield more information when appropriate questions are asked. For instance, the work path within the program operation, the distribution of work load among the program staff, the amount of required paper work, the distribution of program products and/or services, all of these can provide the evaluator with information about costs of the program. Waste can develop within a program activity because the planning process was inadequate or the plans which were formulated for operation procedures were aborted by the program director or workers.

The task of the evaluator is to keep asking questions of the data until he thinks all of the available useful information has been retrieved. The information should be looked at from all sides, the pieces should be separated and reassembled. Reconstruct the program operation from the gathered data and compare with the planned operation. Check for inconsistencies and gaps.

When looking for meaning in the gathered information, the evaluator should use his or her imagination. After the meanings are gleaned then the evaluator should double check to make certain the results are confirmed by the gathered information.

The use of graphs and charts can be useful to more clearly interpret the information. For instance, data about target population level of income, population growth, population shifts, can best be discerned when looked at by means of comparative charts and graphs.

After the gathered information has been interpreted, the results should be checked against the client's criteria for useful information. In this process the evaluator might discover information which could be useful to the client but does not fit the criteria set out by the client. This information should be reported out to the client along with documented reasons why the evaluator believes it to be useful.

Reporting Out the Findings

The form which is to be used in reporting out the findings of the evaluation process should include the background information of the process. It should include the names of the principles involved in the contract, the purpose of the evaluation and the decisions to be made. The evaluator determines what information needs to be depersonalized in order to maintain confidentiality. If graphs, charts, maps, and other pictorial illustrations are to be used they should be clearly presented, that is, the client should be able to read them and know what information is contained within them. Many times the evaluator may find it helpful to use statistics in the evaluation process. When statistics are used in the final report they must be included in such a manner that the client can understand them. The client need not be impressed with the evaluator's skills, he need only be able to have sufficient information to make the needed decisions.

The report-out form should include the method of evaluation used, the processes which have been worked, the instrument used in data gathering, and the persons from whom the data was gathered.

Writing the Final Report

After you have interpreted the data and have made a rough copy of the report-out form, the conclusions which have been drawn from the evaluative material and the recommendations to be presented should be written in the last section of the report. Every conclusion should be documented with two or more cases in point, this is to guard against the evaluator putting his own values into the report.

The alternatives for continuation of the program or replicating the program should be generated for the most part from the information written in the statement of conclusion. These alternatives should be weighted, that is, listed along with expectations in costs and effectiveness.

At this point in the evaluation process the evaluator should share this rough draft with the client for purposes of clarification. The client may say more information is needed in one or two areas which would give more credibility to the suggested alternatives. Or the report may possibly trigger the recall of some information which the client has failed to give the evaluator.

With this new information supplied by the client the evaluator will rewrite the final evaluative report. This final report is delivered to the client.

All gathered data is kept on file by the evaluator until the decisions are made. The data should then be either destroyed or edited to preserve confidentiality and given to the client.

Chapter VIII

CONCLUSION

On the basis of the foregoing presentation, this concluding chapter seeks to advance a few words of advice to would-be evaluators. Evaluation, as viewed by the author, is a data gathering process to produce information for decision making. There are a number of reasons why decision making might take place without giving the evaluation results a hearing. Some of those reasons were listed in an earlier chapter. The evaluator must face reality squarely; that is, evaluation in and of itself is rarely sufficient to bring about change within the organization. However, evaluation can be helpful in bringing about change, and the evaluator can facilitate this change by creating the climate in which change can happen more readily. A review of how this climate creation might take place is now in order.

All persons involved in the program or programs to be evaluated should be participants throughout the entire evaluation process.

The evaluator should be persistent in being as objective as possible, carefully reporting out only documented conclusions and recommendations.

All involved persons should clearly understand what the evaluation process will deliver and the limitations of the process.

The evaluator should be in frequent communication with the involved persons throughout the process.

Even if these conditions are maintained and the final report is clear, precise and well documented no visible results can be guaranteed. For evaluation is a data gathering process and not a decision making process. Although informed decision making may be the sought after goal of a healthy organization the fact remains that many decisions are made apart from accessible information. Decisions are as apt to be emotionally based as they are rationally thought out. Decisions can be, and often are, affected by the history of personal relationships existing within the organization.

In view of the above statements coupled with the amount of work required in a complete evaluation process, the reader might ask: Why bother?

It is important to re-emphasize that the process model of evaluation presented on these pages is derived from the perspective of organizational decision makers and program planners. For the most part these persons have a list of program alternatives from which they must choose the ones to receive resource allocations. They thus see the role of evaluation as a guide to resource allocation. The author views this role as inadequate. It is inadequate because the decision makers and/or program planners have more alternatives than resource allocations, more opportunities for effective programming than increasing or decreasing the funding of existing programs.

The decision maker and/or program planner can add new programs or discontinue existing programs, change the program design with respect to services and/or target population, change the package of programs offered by the organization, as well as reallocating resources among the program.

The author advances the policy of the decision maker and/or program planner sitting down with the evaluator and posing the question: What decisions could be made if one or another result is surfaced by the evaluation process? This exercise could produce a set of hypotheses with directions for program planning. For example, a program might be more effective if people were empowered to seek out their own resources rather than simply supplying these resources.

There are many ways to structure program evaluations. What is being suggested here is that the evaluation process be a collaborative effort involving the decision maker and/or program planner and the evaluator. It is argued here that if this process were followed the quality of evaluation would improve, the relevance of evaluation would increase, and the results of evaluation would be included more in the decision making process.

A Final Note

The evaluation efforts which have been done in church organizations have not been of sufficent quality to have significant impact on the program planning of those organizations. It has been stated that two primary organizational factors, (1) organizational resistance to evaluation, and (2) organizational personnel seeking to find an evaluation process which will support the status quo, contribute to this lack of impact.

However, the evaluators must recognize their role in the ineffectiveness of evaluations with program planning. Not enough effort has been given to relating evaluation to the planning process. Evaluators have not given enough attention to identifying the decisions which must be made from the evaluation data. There has not been sufficient continued interaction between the involved organizational personnel and the evaluator. Evaluation reports are too often only summaries and not analyzed documented reports and, as such, cannot be fully used by the organizational personnel.

The force field created by these two situations, organizational resistance and ineffective evaluation reports, create difficulty for the evaluator. On one side, separation of the evaluation from the program process is required and, on the other side, a closer relationship between the decision maker and/or program planner and the evaluator is called for.

This necessary dichotomy requires the evaluator to use all skills and common sense throughout the process. However, the payoffs have been shown to be worth the effort.

APPENDIX
A SAMPLE EVALUATION REPORT

This report, because of space limitations, is a summary report. The full report would be written in the same form but would include all of the substantiating materials including the interview schedules and questionnaires used in the process. The material which is printed here is included in this writing as a guide to would-be evaluators to aid in the writing up of the process.

Report to
Members of the Administration Division
John Calvin Presbytery

Evaluation of Summer Work Camps
for Minority Youth

Submitted by

Mrs. Dorothy Lynn, Chairperson
The Reverend Franklin Matthews
The Reverend James Myers, Jr.

The Review and Evaluation Task Force
of John Calvin Presbytery

Authorization and Introduction

The John Calvin Presbytery, meeting on February 26, 1976, at Effingham, directed the Review and Evaluation Task Force *"to undertake in the next six months an in-depth evaluation of Presbytery's program: Summer Work Camps for Minority Youth and to report its finding and recommendations to the Administration Division prior to the October, 1976 meeting (of Presbytery)."* **Minutes, February 26, 1976, page 6.**

This study of the Summer work camps was directed for the following purposes:

1. To discover the adequacy of the four camps offered each year to meet the needs of the number of minority youth seeking summer employment.

2. To determine if the goals of these work camps are being met. These goals are stated in the Program Manual of the Presbytery.

3. To determine if the members of the staff are (1) sufficient in number and (2) adequately trained to cope with the unique set of problems encountered.

4. To determine if the organizations, for whom the students are working, feel the work is effective in helping to meet the organizational needs.

There was and remains an unwritten purpose for requesting this evaluation. This purpose, to give a priority rating to this program as compared with the other programs of the Presbytery, is made clear in the next section wherein the problems are delineated.

The evaluation team, following discussions with leaders of Presbytery, has determined this unwritten purpose to be the main purpose and, therefore, has addressed itself to this issue in the following report.

Statement of Problems

The chief concern leading to this evaluation was that of generating substantial information for the decisions to be made concerning the total programming agenda of the Presbytery. In 1975 the Presbytery adopted the practice of using an annual zero-based budget, requiring each of its programs to present substantiating evidence for continuance. This action was precipitated by rising costs of maintenance and programs and the decreasing amount of dollars being pledged to Presbytery by the local churches for the purpose of Presbytery level programming.

For the past several years each local church has been faced with the impact of an inflationary economic trend. Salaries, administration and local programming costs have increased at a rapid pace and the increase of dollars pledged has not kept up. This economic situation has had a negative effect upon the amount of benevolent dollars available to the Presbytery, thus bringing about increased competition between program planners for scarce resources. In this case the scarce resource is dollars.

As these problems were discussed by the Presbytery, many questions were raised about the cost-benefits of all of the programs initiated and carried forth by the Presbytery. They saw inadequate long range planning and a lack of managerial guidance as handicaps to the plans for a more accurate budgeting process. In addition, they expressed concern about programming decisions being made without sufficient and reliable information.

Method

The study was undertaken in the following steps. The initial step was orientation of the evaluators to the organization and to the communities in which the program was being implemented. The second step was to discover how the program was started, what needs were being met, the original program goals and the intended target population. The third step was the design of the evaluation model and the identification of the subjects of the interviews and questionnaires. The fourth step was the gathering of the data, the interpretation and analysis of the gathered data. The fifth step was the writing up of this information in a form to be presented to the Administration Division of the Presbytery.

In the past four years there have been 635 minority youth participants in this program. We sent out 200 questionnaires and received 127 in return. This represents a 63% response. We selected 20 of these respondents for follow-up interviews.

We interviewed 11 part time help, 3 full time presbytery staff persons, and the eleven members of the Outreach Division, the Division in Presbytery which has the oversight of this program.

32 persons, delegates to the meeting of Presbytery, were selected at random and were asked questions concerning their knowledge and feelings about the Minority Work Camps.

We interviewed representatives of the 42 organizations who have been partners with the Presbytery in this program. These organizations were the ones who employed the students during the summer months.

On-site observations were made during this past summer at the locations of the 24 organizations who were participating in this year's program.

The data has been gathered, analyzed and interpreted. This report represents our best understanding and analysis of the evaluative effort.

We realize the usefulness of this report depends on the validity of the information we have gathered and the degree to which we have accurately interpreted this data. There are many variables which impact every program and no evaluation process can lay claim to having surfaced all of them. Therefore, the conclusions reached and reported to you should not be taken as absolute truth but, rather, as the evaluation team's best understanding of what has been taking place in this program's operation. Hopefully, this report will supply sufficient information for you to make the required and informed decisions.

History

The minority Youth Work Camps program was started in the late 1960's as a response to the restlessness of youth exhibited in that decade. The concerns of the people were being focused on the nonavailability of jobs for students who were of the minority races. This first program involved 37 students who were all of the Negro race. The number of participants in this program has steadily increased over the past seven years until the present time when two hundred are working in 24 organizations. The minority groups making up the participant population have changed from being only those of the Negro race to now being 60% Spanish speaking youth, 35% Negro youth, and the other 5% being primarily American Indians with 8 Koreans and 2 Vietnamese.

This program, for the outset, was based on two predominant assumptions: First, minority youth do not have the easy access to cultural and economic systems of the society and, secondly, this entry pattern could be changed if the minority youth could gain work experience and marketable skills.

The original program came into being as the result of the Presbytery approving a proposal submitted by the Social Awareness Task Force (under the present structures of Presbytery this has become the Outreach Division). This proposal called for $10,000 to be used as start up money and to pay for the housing and food of the participants. A member of the existing Presbytery would serve as director of the program and would coordinate all planning and strategy. A Seminary student, if available, was to be employed for the summer months to assist the director in his duties. The program has become a major effort of the Presbytery. A full time staff person has been employed by Presbytery and her sole responsibility is the managing and running of this program. Three Seminary students are employed for the summer months to help the director. The total budget for this program is now (1975) $40,000 per year.

There have been three major crises in the program's seven year history. The first crisis was precipitated when a group of residents raised organized resistance to the housing of blacks in the all white neighborhoods. This crisis was partially met by imposing strict behavioral codes upon the participating youths. By the second year sufficient neighborhood integration had taken place within the communities to allow for placing the minority youths in homes in integrated neighborhoods.

The second crisis came at the beginning of the program's fourth year. The number of requests from students to be participants in the program sharply increased, necessitating a major decision concerning increasing the program budget and staff or to maintain the operation at the then present level. The Presbytery made the decision to increase budget and staff to accomodate the increased requests for participation. There are those members of Presbytery who remain convinced that this decision was an error in judgment.

The third crisis, the current one, is that of less benevolent dollars being available to Presbytery programs. This crisis precipitated the zero-based program budget policy of Presbytery and is the impetus for this evaluation effort.

Findings

There have been 778 participants in the seven years of the program's existence. The following chart shows the break down of participation and the cost per student of the program for each year.

Year	No. of Students	Cost per Student
1969	37	$121.70
1970	46	124.00
1971	60	120.00
1972	111	181.00
1973	126	190.00
1974	198	192.00
1975	200	200.00

Figure 1

One can see that at the beginning of the fourth year, with the additonal staff being added, the cost per student reflected a significant increase. Also the impact of inflation in the last four years has had a telling result.

The questionnaire sent to the student participants of the program was divided into four parts: biographical information, satisfaction with program conditions, how and why the students were involved with the program and students' expectations and realized results.

In order to make the following statistics more meaningful, it is important to note that 95% of those persons who enrolled in the program fulfilled their commitment. Only sixty-eight persons dropped out of the program once they had begun to work.

72% of the students were male and 28% were female. The ages of the students as defined by the program guidelines ranged from fifteen years of age to twenty years of age. The following chart gives the ages of the participants.

No. of Students	Age
172	15
424	16
74	17
22	18
64	19
22	20

Figure 2

As you look at the chart it becomes obvious that the program is reaching those minority youth who are just entering the work period of their lives. From these figures it would appear the program is reaching the intended target population. The one thing lacking in this report is the statistics which would allow us to determine the percentage of the minority youth in the community being reached by this program. There are no such statistics available at this time.

The results of the questionnaires filled out by the students reflected a high level of satisfaction with the program conditions. 70% of the respondents replied that they were able to get work for the summer in an appropriate field. The jobs they were doing in the summer were jobs they thought would be interesting to pursue as a career. Only 5% of the students were very dissatisfied with their summer jobs. 82% replied favorably to the orientation week and said this week was important to them. 12% replied that the orientation week did not adequately prepare them for their particular jobs. 3% said they could have had the same work without the program. Four of these latter respondents reported the only work they got to do was janitor work. It should be noted here that the two organizations for which these four person's worked said these four were assigned to janitorial work because of careless working habits.

As to why the students were involved in the program, the answers were so varied as to allow for no prevalent reason to be cited. If we look at their prior expectations we can see that money was probably the prime motivator. However, the answers given to this section of the questionnaire ranged from parents urging the student to be involved, to the student looking for some action in an otherwise boring summer.

71% of the students heard about the program from participants who were previously involved, 21% from the public school counselors, and the other 8% learned of the program through several different ways.

Approximately 15% of the participants were surprised that they were not turned down after they had applied. They felt this way because of their race.

About 90% of the participants expected to be "preached at" and, of this number 84% were surprised to discover that they were not required to attend church services in order to work in the program.

91% of the students expected to earn money. They had no other expectations for personal gain of the program.

The gains the students felt they received as a result of the program are significant, at least, in the views of the evaluators. 11% of the students are now employed by the same organization for which they worked during the program. 21% replied that the program enabled them to finish high school. 33% felt they had been helped by acquiring skills which would enable them to find work when they had finished high school. 12% could list no specific personal gains as the result of their participation in the program. 22% said available money was the only gain they received from the program.

The feelings of the part-time and full-time staff were all positive. There was a consensus that this program was and remains a worthwhile program for Presbytery to carry on. Each of the staff felt they were a part of a significant contribution being made to society. The edited summaries of the staff interviews are attached to this report. Each of these persons has read the summaries and given permission for the evaluation team to share their remarks with the Administration Division.

Only two of the eleven members of the Outreach Division had been connected with the program from its beginning. Three had served for three years, three had served for two years, and three were in their first year of service. Four of these members were very enthusiastic about the program and had volunteered many hours in support of the staff. Two members felt that although the program was doing some good the Presbytery could no longer afford to continue it. The other five members admitted that they had not been sufficiently involved with the program to give significant input to this study.

The thirty-two delegates to the meeting of Presbytery were hesitant to give input to this report. They felt a lack of knowledge with reference to the program. Twenty-seven were aware of the program taking place and had varying degrees of knowledge about it. Five of the delegates said this interview was the first they had heard of the program. Obviously, the evaluation team's selecting Elder delegates at random was not a fruitful effort. We must report out, though, our surprise at learning that a program which has been continued for seven years and to which 6% of Presbytery's annual budget is committed could evoke such little concern from these delegates.

The forty-two organizations who were partners with John Calvin Presbytery in this program were categorically distributed in the follwing manner as depicted.

CATEGORIES OF ORGANIZATIONS

Category	No. Participating		No. of Students
	1969-75	1975	Employed 1975
Manufacturing	5	5	52 (2)*
Retail Firms	22	11	71 (3)*
Public Schools	7	3	25
Parks and Rec. Dept. of City	1	1	43 (2)*
Service Insti.	6	4	9
TOTAL	41	24	200 (7)*

Seven students dropped out during the first month of the program. Three left because their families moved out of the area and four quit for personal reasons.

Figure 3

Four of the retail firms and one service institution reported they had participated for one year in the program and found it to be unsatisfactory. They reported that their business was such that allowed them to operate with a stable work force and the program was an interruption to that pattern. Two retail firms felt the program was worthwhile but they could not afford to participate.

Thirty-four organizations said the program was beneficial to the community, to the students and to the organizations. There were only seven incidents reported as happening throughout the program to be serious enough to cause concern for the continuation of the program. Two of these incidents were accidents which caused a loss of limb of the participants. Three of the incidents were related to Union concerns and have since been worked out. The other two incidents involved theft. The organizations all said these were problems common to any organization and were not unique to this program. Seventeen representatives from these organizations have written assessments of their involvement with the program and recommendations for future consideration. These assessments are attached to this report.

The planning process and the functional structure of the Summer Work Camps program have been operationally effective. Even though there have been three program directors in the seven years of the program's existence, the evaluators found no evidence of transitional gaps. Each transition from one director to the next was smooth and had no visible adverse effects upon the program operation.

At the beginning of this program, under the directorship of John Ewing, the participating organizations, the Outreach Division members, the community leaders and members of the target population have been a part of the process. There is at present an advisory board consisting of representatives of these five groups.

The effort put into this program has been, and continues to be, directional; the issues have been clearly defined, the goals articulated and the strategy carefully considered. There has been adequate research and study prior to major decisions being made.

The one area which the study surfaced as needing more effort is the area of apprising the Presbytery's constituency of the program and its favorable results.

The evaluation team is not aware of any other comparible programs being operated and, therefore, can not offer statistcs for the comparison of cost per student of this program.

Summary and Recommendations

John Calvin Presbytery has had a history of being an organization with a strong tradition of community service. It has met the challenge of a rapidly growing population within its bounds. This is evidenced by the new church developments, strong membership recruitment programs, participation in ecumenical ventures and the social action programs all of which are initiated and carried forth by the Presbytery. The Presbytery has now reached a critical stage in its organizational life. That stage is characterized by the high organizational costs, the constituency having to cope with a seemingly endless inflation spiral, and the accompanying intense competition for scarce resources, primarily scarce monies.

We believe the program to be effectively and efficiently run. The data we have gathered would support this conclusion. The only recommendation we would make concerning the program itself is that of informing the members of Presbytery of the progress and results being realized with the program.

As we have noticed earlier the present crisis arises from a lack of funding dollars and not from any weakness in the structure or operation of the Summer Work Camps program. We recommend the continuation of this program and offer several alternatives for acquiring the necessary funding.

1. In view of the way this program is received by the business community and the benefits each organization derives from the program, it is suggested that additional funds be sought out from these partners. This alternative would have the least effect upon the present structure. These people are already involved in the planning and operation of the program.

2. A task force be created to explore the possibility of additional funding being secured from the denominational agentry. This alternative would probably require some new guidelines being

imposed upon a smooth running operation. Although the history of such denominational grants does not record a pattern of interference in the local programs.

3. There is a strong possibility that if the city would assume responsibility for this program federal and state funds might become available. This move would effectively take the control of the program out of the hands of the Presbytery. This alternative would allow the monies of Presbytery to be available for new community programs.

4. The fourth alternative is to reduce the program in proportion to the reduced budget of Presbytery. If additional funding cannot be secured this is the alternative which the evaluation team recommends to follow.

5. The fifth alternative would be to cut the program back to be a simple clearing house for job opportunities and available job-seeking youth. It is the opinion of the evaluators that this alternative would wipe out the effectiveness of the present program.

We realize the difficult decisions the Presbytery is facing. It is the hope of the task force that the information generated by this report will be helpful in reaching the necessary decisions. Perhaps, the data can trigger alternatives in the minds of others and will point to appropriate directions which will be mutually beneficial for this program and the total program agenda of the Presbytery.

We wish to express our gratitude for every one who has helped us to complete this process. The cooperation made our task much easier.

BIBLIOGRAPHY

Bauer, R.A.,ed. Social Indicators, MIT Press, Cambridge, MA:1966.

Bennis, W., Benne, K.D., and Chin R. The Planning of Change, Holt, Rinehart & Winston, Inc. New York: 1969.

Davis, J. A. Elementary Survey Analysis, Prentice-Hall, Englewood Cliffs, N. J.: 1971.

Gordon, R. L. Interviewing Strategy, Techniques and Tactics, The Dorsey Press, Homewood, IL: 1969.

Hall, Richard. Organizations: Structure and Process, Prentice-Hall, Englewood Cliffs, N. J.: 1972.

Herzberg, Frederick, Job Attitudes: Research and Opinion, Psychological Service, Pittsburgh: 1957.

Katz, Daniel and Kahn, Robert, The Social Psychology of Organizations, Wiley, New York: 1966.

Likert, R. and Likert, J. G. New Ways of Managing Conflict, McGraw-Hill, New York: 1976.

McGregor, Douglas, Leadership and Motivation, MIT Press, Cambridge, MA: 1966.

Miller, D. C. Handbook of Research Design and Social Measurement, David McKay & Co., N. Y.: New York: 1964.

DATE DUE

DEC 1 2 1980			
FEB 4 1981			
FEB 17 1981			
APR 2 7			
SEP 21			
NOV 9			

DEMCO 38-297

Rossi, P   ng
  Social   .

Schindle
  Volun
  Washi   ,

Steers, R
  Effecti   976

Suchmar
  Sage F

Tagiuri,
  Organi
  Boston

Van Man   tion,
  Nation
  Washi   ,

Vroom V
  Univer

Warren,
  Press,

Webb, E. J., Campbell, D. T., Schwartz, R. D. and
  Secrest, L. B. Unobtrusive Measures: Nonreactive
  Measures in the Social Sciences, Rand McNally
  and Co., Chicago: 1966.

Weiss, C. H., Evaluation Research: Methods
  of Assessing Program Effectiveness, Prentice-
  Hall, Inc. Englewood Cliffs, N. J.: 1972.